GRIFFIN POETRY PRIZE
Anthology 2023

Published in Canada and the USA in 2023 by House of Anansi Press Inc.
houseofanansi.com

House of Anansi Press is committed to protecting our natural environment.
This book is made of material from well-managed FSC®-certified forests, recycled materials,
and other controlled sources.

House of Anansi Press is a Global Certified Accessible™ (GCA by Benetech) publisher.
The ebook version of this book meets stringent accessibility standards and is available to
readers with print disabilities.

27 26 25 24 23   1 2 3 4 5

Library and Archives Canada Cataloguing in Publication

Cataloguing data available from Library and Archives Canada

Cover design: Kyra Griffin and Chloé Griffin
Cover artwork: Gwenaël Rattke, *Vue imaginaire d'une fenêtre*, 2022,
silkscreen & collage on paper, 29.75" x 21.75". Care of Romer Young Gallery.

Every reasonable effort has been made to trace ownership of copyright materials.
The publisher will gladly rectify any inadvertent errors or omissions in credits in future editions.
Please contact info@griffinpoetryprize.com.

*House of Anansi Press is grateful for the privilege to work on and create from the Traditional Territory
of many Nations, including the Anishinabeg, the Wendat, and the Haudenosaunee, as well as the
Treaty Lands of the Mississaugas of the Credit.*

Canada Council   Conseil des Arts
for the Arts   du Canada

ONTARIO ARTS COUNCIL
CONSEIL DES ARTS DE L'ONTARIO
an Ontario government agency
un organisme du gouvernement de l'Ontario

With the participation of the Government of Canada
Avec la participation du gouvernement du Canada

Canadä

*We acknowledge for their financial support of our publishing program the Canada Council
for the Arts, the Ontario Arts Council, and the Government of Canada.*

Printed and bound in Canada

GRIFFIN POETRY PRIZE

Anthology 2023

A SELECTION OF THE SHORTLIST

Edited by GREGORY SCOFIELD

ANANSI

2001

International
Yehuda Amichai
  Translated by Chana Bloch and
  Chana Kronfeld
Paul Celan
  Translated by Nikolai Popov
  and Heather McHugh
Fanny Howe
Les Murray

Canadian
Anne Carson
Ghandl of the Qayahl Llaanas
  Translated by Robert
  Bringhurst
Don McKay

2002

International
Victor Hernández Cruz
Christopher Logue
Les Murray
Alice Notley

Canadian
Christian Bök
Erín Moure
Karen Solie

2003

International
Kathleen Jamie
Paul Muldoon
Gerald Stern
C. D. Wright

Canadian
Margaret Avison
Dionne Brand
P. K. Page

2004

International
Suji Kwock Kim
David Kirby
August Kleinzahler
Louis Simpson

Canadian
Di Brandt
Leslie Greentree
Anne Simpson

2005

International
Fanny Howe
Michael Symmons Roberts
Matthew Rohrer
Charles Simic

Canadian
Roo Borson
George Bowering
Don McKay

2006

International
Kamau Brathwaite
Durs Grünbein
  Translated by Michael
  Hofmann
Michael Palmer
Dunya Mikhail
  Translated by Elizabeth
  Winslow

Canadian
Phil Hall
Sylvia Legris
Erín Moure

2007

International
Paul Farley
Rodney Jones
Frederick Seidel
Charles Wright

Canadian
Ken Babstock
Don McKay
Priscila Uppal

2008

International
John Ashbery
Elaine Equi
César Vallejo
  Translated by Clayton
  Eshleman
David Harsent

Canadian
Robin Blaser
Nicole Brossard
  Translated by Robert Majzels
  and Erín Moure
David W. McFadden

2009

International
Mick Imlah
Derek Mahon
C. D. Wright
Dean Young

Canadian
Kevin Connolly
Jeramy Dodds
A. F. Moritz

2010

International
John Glenday
Louise Glück
Eiléan Ní Chuilleanáin
Valérie Rouzeau
    Translated by Susan Wicks

Canadian
Kate Hall
P. K. Page
Karen Solie

2011

International
Seamus Heaney
Adonis
    Translated by Khaled Mattawa
François Jacqmin
    Translated by Philip Mosley
Gjertrud Schnackenberg

Canadian
Dionne Brand
Suzanne Buffam
John Steffler

2012

International
David Harsent
Yusef Komunyakaa
Sean O'Brien
Tadeusz Różewicz
    Translated by Joanna Trzeciak

Canadian
Ken Babstock
Phil Hall
Jan Zwicky

2013

International
Ghassan Zaqtan
    Translated by Fady Joudah
Jennifer Maiden
Alan Shapiro
Brenda Shaughnessy

Canadian
David W. McFadden
James Pollock
Ian Williams

2014

International
Rachael Boast
Brenda Hillman
Carl Phillips
Tomasz Różycki
    Translated by Mira Rosenthal

Canadian
Anne Carson
Sue Goyette
Anne Michaels

2015

International
Wang Xiaoni
    Translated by Eleanor Goodman
Wioletta Grzegorzewska
    Translated by Marek
    Kazmierski
Michael Longley
Spencer Reece

Canadian
Shane Book
Jane Munro
Russell Thornton

2016

International
Norman Dubie
Joy Harjo
Don Paterson
Rowan Ricardo Phillips

Canadian
Ulrikka S. Gernes
    Translated by Per Brask and
    Patrick Friesen
Liz Howard
Soraya Peerbaye

2017

International
Jane Mead
Abdellatif Laâbi
    Translated by Donald
    Nicholson-Smith
Alice Oswald
Denise Riley

Canadian
Jordan Abel
Hoa Nguyen
Sandra Ridley

2018

International
Tongo Eisen-Martin
Susan Howe
Layli Long Soldier
Natalie Shapero

Canadian
Billy-Ray Belcourt
Aisha Sasha John
Donato Mancini

2019

International
Raymond Antrobus
Daniel Borzutzky
Kim Hyesoon
Translated by Don Mee Choi
Luljeta Lleshanaku
Translated by Ani Gjika

Canadian
Dionne Brand
Eve Joseph
Sarah Tolmie

2020

International
Abigail Chabitnoy
Sharon Olds
Etel Adnan
Translated by Sarah Riggs
Natalie Scenters-Zapico

Canadian
Chantal Gibson
Doyali Farah Islam
Kaie Kellough

2021

International
Victoria Chang
Valzhyna Mort
Srikanth Reddy
Yi Lei
Translated by Tracy K. Smith
and Changtai Bi

Canadian
Joseph Dandurand
Canisia Lubrin
Yusuf Saadi

2022

International
Gemma Gorga
Translated by Sharon Dolin
Douglas Kearney
Natalka Bilotserkivets
Translated by Ali Kinsella and
Dzvinia Orlowsky
Ed Roberson

Canadian
David Bradford
Liz Howard
Tolu Oloruntoba

CONTENTS

PREFACE

The most beautiful thing a poet can offer us—gift us—is the passage, the journey into their world of love and loss, chaos and peace, brutality and compassion, and the hope there is language to articulate what most cannot say or allow themselves to contemplate.

The poet is a visionary, a dreamer, a builder, who, in the moments between stillness and cacophony, creates for us a foundation, a house in which we can take rest from a world where we've been taught not to listen, not to touch that which makes us fragile and yet so beautifully strong, so beautifully capable. The poet is a visionary who clears the path before we know it exists. The poet is a dreamer who dreams us into existence. And the poet is a carpenter who creates for us a home in this place we call *Ourselves*. This place where we attempt to make sense of the things we're constantly unpacking: the teacups of hope, the plates of understanding, the linens draping our bones—the very things that poets, the visionaries, call us to examine in the stillness of the page, the frame of a stanza, the utterance of a word that becomes a room, a dwelling, a home.

The boxes of poetry books for this year's Griffin Poetry Prize began to arrive in August 2022. They continued to arrive throughout October and December, and January 2023, for a total of 602 books. The books represented poets and countries from around the world, a number of them translated into English from Greek, Spanish, Mandarin, and Arabic, to name a few. Still other books represented a vast array of geographies and racial-cultural experiences, political histories and histories of colonial occupation and genocide, histories of settlement and resettlement, family and community histories, songs and stories of home and place, land and country. There were stories of personal grief and devastation, the many falling petals of those losses, as well as stories of love and hope, the many blooms of those most wondrous moments. There were stories of resistance and courage and the sheer stubbornness of the human heart. There were stories of pain and triumph. There were stories of anger and confusion, resilience and celebration—but stories that always led us to a new light. A new home. A new vision that unfolded as I moved from page to page, from book to book, transported to countries and homes I'll likely never visit. Each collection of poetry symbolized a new career or a lifelong work. Each book, a perfect visitor, shared my armchair, table, or bed, calling me far from myself and far from my own small world. And each book, a different fire, left me shifting from darkness to light, a certain light that is only given to the poets. To the poets this light is born. To this light is born the poet.

And so comes the question: How does one choose a longlist of ten books, a shortlist of five books, a winner from 602 books, each of them a brilliant fire? How does one choose the brightest fire, the warmest one? The one that is exemplary? The one that is most extraordinary? The one that needs to be seen by the world?

The Griffin Poetry Prize is perhaps the largest, most prestigious award I've been asked to adjudicate. Truth be told, had I known the amount of work involved, I may have reconsidered the invitation. I didn't realize the volume of books I would need to pore over, the research involved, and, of course, the difficult decisions I and my fellow jurors would have to make. From past experience, I'm well aware juries can go many different ways—some of them sideways, unfortunately. There is usually a lot at stake, namely prize money and recognition. Recognition that is so incredibly important for a poet. This poet, who is born with a certain light—perhaps, one can say, a sacred light.

Nonetheless, I'm incredibly pleased that I accepted the invitation. Meeting weekly or monthly with my fellow jurors, incredible poets themselves, Nikola Madzirov (Macedonia) and Natasha Trethewey (USA), was an absolute delight. Out of the 602 submissions, we most often found common fires, poets whose books gifted us light long after we'd read them. And so, in the end, it was about light. It was about the light we wanted to share with the world, and the poets, who were born into this light. This sacred light. This light that guides us home to *Ourselves*.

I hope you enjoy the poets featured in the following pages. Each poem is a gift of light. Each poem comes from the dream-time, the one before first dawn.

With warmest wishes.
kinanâskomtinawâw,
Gregory Scofield, Victoria, April 2023

GRIFFIN POETRY PRIZE
Anthology 2023

ROBYN CRESWELL

TRANSLATED FROM THE ARABIC WRITTEN BY IMAN MERSAL

The Threshold

The Threshold by Iman Mersal is a powerful collection of poetry that dissects the fluid architecture of identity, hidden memory, and language. Mersal, an Egyptian-Canadian poet and writer living in Edmonton, Alberta, weaves together personal experiences, cultural references, and philosophical musings to create a vivid and eloquent poetic narrative. The poems in *The Threshold*, translated beautifully by Robyn Creswell, are deeply personal, reflecting the loss of her father, and her struggles with displacement and belonging, as she navigates different cultures and languages. She says that these poems mark the end of an era in her life and her relation to Cairo, the moment of leaving the life she knows behind: "A walk in Cairo, tracing its topography, becomes an elegy, as well as a celebration of the beloved city." When Mersal left Egypt for the first time, an aunt who had never left her home province sent her off with an Egyptian expression: "May it be a happy threshold." *The Threshold* is a place of rebirth where one must undergo a ritual or transformation in order to cross over into a new world, a new horizon of life, and new borders of awakening.

Just sleeping

His lips twist in anger
at something he no longer remembers.
He sleeps deeply,
hands under his head,
like the conscripts of Central Security
in their late-night trucks,
eyes closed against all they've seen,
breathing in sync with the engines,
transformed all at once into angels.

Visits

My dead mother often visits in dreams,
sometimes wiping from my nose what she thinks is school
    yard dirt,
sometimes doing my braids
with tough and practiced hands,
unable to see the scissors
that later subjugated my unruly hair
and blind to its hacked-off ends.

You too
might stop the world's turning when you die,
which would give me enough time
to point all this out to you.

Little lockers

Typically, windows are gray
and generously proportioned,
allowing those in bed
to follow the traffic
and weather conditions outside.

Typically, doctors have aquiline noses
and spectacles
that establish the distance between them and pain.

Typically, relatives leave roses
at the room's entrance
asking forgiveness from the dead-to-be.

Typically, women wander the hallways
without makeup
while sons stand under bright lights
clutching X-rays
and promising to stop their spitefulness
if only their parents are granted a little more time.

Everything repeats itself.
The little lockers fill up with new bodies
like a perforated lung, inhaling the world's oxygen
and leaving all these other chests
to suck the wind.

It seems I inherit the dead

After I walked back among all the large shoes
from my mother's burial
leaving her to tend her chickens in some obscurer place
it was my job to protect our house from the neighbors' spying
and I got used to sitting on the doorstep
waiting for the heroine—the one they always treated badly—
of the radio serials.
The day my friend received a visa
to try out her body on a foreign continent
(and although she hadn't forgotten, as she usually did,
her cigarettes on my table)
I decided that smoking was henceforth necessary
and soon I had a private drawer
and also a mysterious man
who was in fact my friend's former lover.

Also
when doctors fail to find a kidney
Osama's body doesn't reject—
Osama,
whose kidneys shrivel
because he represses his bitterness for the sake of elegance—
then I might use his thumbprint
while talking to prove I'm here.

It seems I inherit the dead,
and one day
I'll sit by myself in a café
after the death of all those I loved
without any feeling of loss
because my body is a large woven basket
where they have left
their traces.

They tear down my family home

As if sledgehammers weren't enough
the demolition men use their hands
to tear down the window djinn used to flit through
and with a kick the back door is gone. Its memory is gone.
Underfoot I feel the remains of the sugar loaves, oranges, and
    mangoes
our furtive visitors hid under their black shawls.
They would come after evening prayer, the hems of their long
    jalabiyas
brushing across the threshold of the back door,
a door of gifts and sorceresses, now a door to nowhere.
The roof that never protected my childhood from the delta rains
has reverted to its old self—a few trees you can count on one
    hand.

Now they're tearing down her old bedroom, casting into the air
strands of her still-wet hair, hair that flies up from the cracks
of earthen walls about to become clods of dirt,
as if no one had ever rested their back there.
Did my mother bathe before bed or at dawn?
Did she pull her hair from the comb's teeth to ward off
the evil eye, or fire, or the stratagems of neighbors?
My mother's hair slips away like a gift, or retribution.
What ties me to her now?
I donated her dresses to charity because they didn't fit me.
If we met, I'd be her older sister.
What ties me to her now? Her womb is with her in the
    ground—there
under the camphor tree, where early death is close enough to
    touch with your hand.

Why did she come?

Why did she come to the New World? This mummy, this
    curiosity,
lying in state in her dusty linen, stuffed with life behind the
    museum's glass.
Maybe mummification is the opposite of immortality
since no mummy will ever animate a rose.
The mummy didn't choose to emigrate, unlike those who wait
on long lines in embassies, build homes in foreign countries,
and dream of returning once they've turned into corpses.
You must take us back
is the legacy they hang around their children's necks
as if death were an identity
that can't be claimed until you're in the family plot.

                                    *

Here too there are green trees, stooped under the weight of
    snow,
and also rivers—though no lovers embrace on their banks,
thronged instead on Sunday mornings by joggers and their dogs
who never pause to look at the water, rigid with loneliness—
and immigrants unschooled as nature lovers but convinced that
    pollution
levels are lower here and that chewing gelatin capsules of
    oxygen before bed
will lead to a longer life.

                                    *

Why can't they forget they're from there?
These wretched outsiders
training their mouth muscles to disguise their accents—
accents like inherited diseases, exposing them
as soon as they get angry

and forget how to express their griefs in a foreign tongue.
Accents don't die but emigrants are good gravediggers.
They hang the names of dead family on the fridge
so as not to telephone them by mistake
and they pay a quarter of their salary on phone bills
to prove they live in a place very far from their childhood.
Why can't they forget?

*

The organic food is still unpurchased yet for the last hour
I've been staring at a photo of my mother sitting on the
    doorstep
of her father's house, which no longer exists—
I mean the doorstep, though my mother doesn't either.
There's no one on the sidewalk. Cars come and go by remote
    control.
I bought this house with its vestigial doorstep
from the widow of a Spanish sculptor who built it on land
leased from Ukrainian emigrants whom the Canadian
    government gave it to
after expropriating it from aboriginal peoples to construct a city
with several universities, dozens of shopping malls,
and thousands like me who own remote-control cars
and understand the health benefits of *aliments biologiques*.

*

In just six steps, the lonely emigrant writes a model letter to his
    family:
—he chooses a moment when he isn't missing them
—he sits with his back to the street since walls are more neutral
—he carefully distributes his *salaams*
—he recites the formulas he was raised on and never expected to
    repeat, such as *I love you more than there are stars in the sky*

or grains of sand by the shore and *I dream of you as the thirsty*
man dreams of water and the sick man dreams of a cure and
the stranger of his homeland
—he says nothing of his actual life since he isn't sure how it
   might be received
—he writes *thank God* many times to assure them of his faith

*

What you've learned here is no different from what you learned
   there:
—reading is a passport away from reality
—hide anxiety with vulgar language
—banish weakness by growing your nails
—handle insomnia by smoking always and tidying your
   drawers sometimes
—use three different brands of eyedrops to clear your vision,
   then enjoy your blindness (even better is the moment when
   your eyelids close over the burn)
Here as well as there
life seems to exist only to be watched from afar.

*

A surprising peace enters your body.
Just let your head rest beneath the water.
Why not? This is your bright idea, glistening like a pearl in the
   trash?
How can you throw it away like this?
Because it's your own idea, distinct from you, but authentic.
These seconds don't pass one after another,
they are the razor's edge between moments.
You remember the dirty dishes in the kitchen, the mail with
   its catalogs,
the lights drilling into your eyes ...

The mercy you didn't know you were looking for is here. It will
    slip into your lungs
if you let your body relax...sink to the bottom...stay down
    just a few seconds more...
There's no reason to be frightened.
Time makes no difference.
It isn't a weight dragging your courage down.
Time is nothing, time is just time.

*

You left your poor enemies on another continent
and feel ashamed whenever you think of them.
Nothing makes you angry anymore.
It's hard to meet a classical Communist here, where clocks
hang in government offices rather than pictures of the
    president.
Perhaps these days of sedation are the real nightmare.
Nothing here deserves your rebellion.
You are content and you are dead.
The life around you is like the hand of mercy
turning up the room lights for an old blind man
so he can read the past.

CV

A ruthless catalog of sorrows:
years in front of the screen, diplomas before jobs,
and languages—all that torture—now ranged under *Languages*.
Where are all the wasted days? And the nights
of walking with hands stretched out
and the visions that crept over the walls?
Where are the feelings of guilt
and the sudden sadness faced with a little hill of fruit
atop a handcart in some forgotten street?
Years with no mention of the empty hours or the funerals,
expunged of black depressions and nibbled nails,
the house keys forgotten inside the house.
There isn't a single open window
and no trace of the desire, deferred, to leap out.
A life overstuffed with accomplishments,
scrubbed free of dirt:
proof that the one who lived it
has cut all ties to the earth.

The book of desire

With his hand
by my hair
a man pulled me up
when I was drowning after walking
on water
an ark made of gold split in two
with a forest in the middle
and a sun that was like the sun
a cinerous wave of velvet but no ashes
a museum for everything extinct
and still deeper down
tiny fish swam into my lungs
and by my hair
with his hand
a man pulled me up until I twisted in the wind
time streamed past
and the mountains wavered between flames and light
all this happened and then I was back onshore
my dress torn
feeling the sand's firmness
and now that I'm here
    I'm not frightened of the sea
    for the closed book of desire
    is open
    with a bookmark on one of its pages.

ADA LIMÓN

The Hurting Kind

Again and again the clarity of vision and depth of emotion in this lovely book turns the ordinary on its head, asking us to slow down, to see the world askew, and thus anew. Tinged with grief and longing, and buoyed by wonder in the natural world and the possibility of human connection, these are poems that seem to move effortlessly—in the way that only a deft touch can do. The precision of syntax—at once plainspoken and fiercely lyrical—unfolds its revelations masterfully and with a kind of grace that is often heartbreaking. *The Hurting Kind* is a marvel.

Give Me This

I thought it was the neighbor's cat, back
to clean the clock of the fledgling robins low
in their nest stuck in the dense hedge by the house,
but what came was much stranger, a liquidity
moving, all muscle and bristle: a groundhog
slippery and waddle-thieving my tomatoes, still
green in the morning's shade. I watched her
munch and stand on her haunches, taking such
pleasure in the watery bites. Why am I not allowed
delight? A stranger writes to request my thoughts
on suffering. Barbed wire pulled out of the mouth,
as if demanding that I kneel to the trap of coiled
spikes used in warfare and fencing. Instead,
I watch the groundhog more closely and a sound escapes
me, a small spasm of joy I did not imagine
when I woke. She is a funny creature and earnest,
and she is doing what she can to survive.

Forsythia

At the cabin in Snug Hollow near McSwain Branch creek, just spring, all the animals are out, and my beloved and I are lying in bed in a soft silence. We are talking about how we carry so many people with us wherever we go, how, even when simply living, these unearned moments are a tribute to the dead. We are both expecting to hear an owl as the night deepens. All afternoon, from the porch, we watched an Eastern towhee furiously build her nest in the untamed forsythia with its yellow spilling out into the horizon. I told him that the way I remember the name *forsythia* is that when my stepmother, Cynthia, was dying, that last week, she said lucidly but mysteriously, *More yellow.* And I thought yes, more yellow, and nodded because I agreed. Of course, more yellow. And so now in my head, when I see that yellow tangle, I say, *For Cynthia, for Cynthia, forsythia, forsythia, more yellow.* It is night now, and the owl never comes. Only more of night, and what repeats in the night.

The First Fish

When I pulled that great fish up out of Lake Skinner's
    mirrored-double surface, I wanted to release
the tugging beast immediately. Disaster on the rod,
    it seemed he might yank the whole aluminum skiff
down toward the bottom of his breathless world.
    The old tree of a man yelled to hang on and would
not help me as I reeled and reeled, finally seeing
    the black carp come up to meet me, black eye
to black eye. In the white cooler it looked so impossible.
    Is this where I am supposed to apologize? Not
only to the fish, but to the whole lake, land, not only for me
    but for the generations of plunder and vanish.
I remember his terrible mouth opening as if to swallow
    the barbarous girl he'd lose his life to. That gold-ringed
eye did not pardon me, no absolution, no reprieve.
    I wanted to catch something; it wanted to live.
We never ate the bottom-feeder, buried by the rosebush
    where my ancestors swore the roses bloomed
twice as big that year, the year I killed a thing because
    I was told to, the year I met my twin and buried
him without weeping so I could be called brave.

It's the Season I Often Mistake

Birds for leaves, and leaves for birds.
The tawny yellow mulberry leaves
are always goldfinches tumbling
across the lawn like extreme elation.
The last of the maroon crabapple
ovates are song sparrows that tremble
all at once. And today, just when I
could not stand myself any longer,
a group of field sparrows, which were
actually field sparrows, flew up into
the bare branches of the hackberry
and I almost collapsed: leaves
reattaching themselves to the tree
like a strong spell for reversal. What
else did I expect? What good
is accuracy amidst the perpetual
scattering that unspools the world.

The Hurting Kind

I.

On the plane I have a dream I've left half my
    torso on the back porch with my beloved. I have to go

back for it, but it's too late, I'm flying
    and there's only half of me.

Back in Texas, the flowers I've left on
    the counter (I stay alone there so the flowers
are more than flowers) have wilted and knocked over the glass.

At the funeral parlor with my mother, we are holding her father's suit,
    and she says, *He'll swim in these.*

For a moment, I'm not sure what she means,

until I realize she means the clothes are too big.

I go with her like a shield in case they try to upsell her
    the ridiculously ornate urn, the elaborate body box.

It is a nice bathroom in the funeral parlor,
    so I take the opportunity to change my tampon.

When I come out my mother says,
Did you have to change your tampon?

And it seems, all at once, a vulgar life. Or not
    vulgar, but not simple, either.

I'm driving her now to Hillside Cemetery where we meet
    with Rosie, who is so nice we want her to work
everywhere. Rosie as my dentist. Rosie as my president.

My shards are showing, I think. But I do not know what I mean
so I fix my face in the rearview, a face with thousands
      of headstones behind it. Minuscule flags, plastic flowers.

      You can't sum it up, my mother says as we are driving,
and the electronic voice says, *Turn left onto Wildwood Canyon Road*,

so I turn left, happy for the instructions.

Tell me where to go. Tell me how to get there.

She means a life, of course. You cannot sum it up.

2.

A famous poet said he never wanted to hear
another poem about a grandmother or a grandfather.

I imagine him with piles of faded yolk-colored paper,
overloaded with loops of swooping cursive, anemic lyrics

misspelling *mourning* and *morning*. But also, before they arrive,
there's a desperate hand scribbling a memory, following

the cat of imagination into each room. What is lineage,
if not a gold thread of pride and guilt? *She did what?*

Once, when I thought I had decided not to have children,
a woman said, *But who are you to kill your own bloodline?*

I told my friend D that, and she said, *What if you want to kill
your own bloodline, like it's your job?*

In the myth of La Llorona, she drowns her children
to destroy her cheating husband. But maybe she was just tired.

After her husband of seventy-six years has died, my grandmother
(yes, I said it, *grandmother, grandmother*) leans to me and says,

Now teach me poetry.

3.

Sticky packs of photographs,
heteromaniacal postcards.

The war.   The war.   The war.
Bikini girls, tight curls, the word *gams*.

Land boom. Atchison, Topeka,
and the Santa Fe. Southern Pacific.

We ask my grandma Allamay
about her mother, for a form.

Records and wills. Evidence of life.
For a moment she can't remember
her mother's maiden name.

She says, *Just tell them she never
wanted me. That should be enough.*

*Red sadness is the secret
one*, writes Ruefle. Redlands

was named after the soil.
Allamay can still
hold a peach in her hand

and judge its number by
its size. Tell you where it
would go in the box

if you're packing peaches
for a living. Which she did,

though she hated the way
the hairs hurt her hands.

4.

Why do we quickly dismiss our ancient ones? Before our phones
        stole the light of our faces, shiny and blue in the televised night,

they worked farms and butchered and trapped animals and swept houses
        and returned to each other after long hours and told stories.

In order for someone to be "good" do they have to have
        seen the full-tilt world? Must they believe what we believe?

My grandmother keeps a picture of her president in the top drawer
        of her dresser, and once, when she was delusional, she dreamt

he had sent my grandfather and her on a trip to Italy. *He paid for it all*,
        she kept repeating.

That same night, on her ride to the hospital, she talks to the medical
        technician and says,

All my grandchildren are Mexican.

She says so proudly; she repeats it to me on the phone.

5.

Once, a long time ago, we sat in the carport of my grandparents'
        house in Redlands, now stolen by eminent domain,

now the hospital parking lot, no more coyotes or caves
        where the coyotes would live, or the grandfather clock

in the house my grandfather built, the porch above the orchard,
        all gone.

We sat in the carport and watched the longest snake
        I'd ever seen undulate between the hanging succulents.

They told me not to worry, that the snake had a name,

        the snake was called a California king,

all slick black with yellow
        stripes like wonders wrapping around him.

My grandparents, my ancestors, told me never
        to kill a California king, benevolent

as they were, equanimous like earth or sky, not

        toothy like the dog Chacho who barked
at nearly every train whistle or roadrunner.

Before my grandfather died, I asked him what sort
        of horse he had growing up. He said,

Just a horse. My horse, with such a tenderness it
        rubbed the bones in my ribs all wrong.

I have always been too sensitive, a weeper
        from a long line of weepers.

I am the hurting kind. I keep searching for proof.

My grandfather carried that snake to the cactus,
        where all sharp things could stay safe.

6.

You can't sum it up. A life.

I feel it moving through me, that snake,
        his horse Midge sturdy and nothing special,

traveling the canyons and the tumbleweeds
        hunting for rabbits before the war.

My grandmother picking peaches. Stealing
        the fruit from the orchards as she walked

home. No one said it was my job to remember.

        I took no notes, though I've stared too long.
My grandfather, before he died, would have told

        anyone that could listen that he was ordinary,

that his life was a good one, simple, he could never
        understand why anyone would want to write

it down. He would tell you straight up he wasn't
brave. And my grandmother would tell you right now

that he is busy getting the house ready for her. Visiting now
each night and even doing the vacuuming.

I imagine she's right. It goes on and on, their story.
          They met in first grade in a one-room schoolhouse,

I could have started their story there, but it
          is endless and ongoing. All of this

is a conjuring. I will not stop this reporting of attachments.
          There is evidence everywhere.

There's a tree over his grave now, and soon her grave too

          though she is tough and says, *If I ever die,*

which is marvelous and maybe why she's still alive.

I see the tree above the grave and think, *I'm wearing*

my heart on my leaves. My heart on my leaves.

Love ends. But what if it doesn't?

Against Nostalgia

If I had known, back then, you were coming,
when I first thought love could be the thing
to save me after all—if I had known, would I
have still glued myself to the back of his
motorcycle while we flew across the starless
bridge over the East River to where I grew
my first garden behind the wire fencing,
in the concrete raised beds lined by ruby
twilight roses? If I had known it would be you,
who even then I liked to look at, across a room,
always listening rigorously, a self-questioning look,
the way your mouth was always your mouth,
would I have climbed back on that bike again
and again until even I was sick with fumes
and the sticky seat too hot in the early fall?
If I had known, would I have still made mistake
after mistake until I had only the trunk of me
left, stripped and nearly bare of leaves?
If I had known, the truth is, I would have kneeled
and said, *Sooner, come to me sooner.*

The End of Poetry

Enough of osseous and chickadee and sunflower
and snowshoes, maple and seeds, samara and shoot,
enough chiaroscuro, enough of thus and prophecy
and the stoic farmer and faith and our father and 'tis
of thee, enough of bosom and bud, skin and god
not forgetting and star bodies and frozen birds,
enough of the will to go on and not go on or how
a certain light does a certain thing, enough
of the kneeling and the rising and the looking
inward and the looking up, enough of the gun,
the drama, and the acquaintance's suicide, the long-lost
letter on the dresser, enough of the longing and
the ego and the obliteration of ego, enough
of the mother and the child and the father and the child
and enough of the pointing to the world, weary
and desperate, enough of the brutal and the border,
enough of can you see me, can you hear me, enough
I am human, enough I am alone and I am desperate,
enough of the animal saving me, enough of the high
water, enough sorrow, enough of the air and its ease,
I am asking you to touch me.

SUSAN MUSGRAVE

Exculpatory Lilies

The sheer humanity and gift to show our fragile, broken selves is nothing less than prayer, as spoken in Musgrave's *Exculpatory Lilies*. That she brings us to the sacred ground of loss and grief, and then lifts us toward our own humility is a ceremony. A ceremony wherein we must bow down our heads to the fragility of all we know, the darkness and light we all must carry.

The True Beginning of Loneliness

is the moment before you are born, the moment
you hesitate to reconsider before your head
crowns. I know. And your second thought
might have been, *isn't it enough that the arrow
fit into the wound it makes?* but by then
it was far too late. Years later, when I had come
to believe loneliness is what I had been born to,
I watched a master of Zen archery fit an arrow
to his bow. He'd set up his target at the edge
of a cliff, where he took careful aim. The arrow
sailed high over the target, and plunged
into the sea. The teacher looked at me,
his inquisitive student, and shouted
                                    bullseye!
all I would ever need to know.

Postscript
September 14, 2021

The day you are cremated, a girl modelling a black hoodie
like the one I've chosen for you to wear, lights up my Facebook page:
I survived because the fire inside me burned brighter than the fire
around me. I hear you laugh at the irony as they fire up the retort,
a laugh dragged through the ashes of a thousand cigarettes, tokes
of crack, my sweet dangerous reckless girl, what could I do
but weep, the way I did when you were four, butting out
a Popeye candy cigarette you scored from the boy next door
for showing him your vagina through the split cedar fence.
I told you, *next time, baby, hold out for a whole pack*, trying
to be brave, the way only a mother could. Now I carry you home
in a plain cedar urn, the remains of all you once were reduced
to this smaller, portable size. Not even you would survive
the fire this time, your light in ashes now, formless as the divine.

The Way Water Sleeps

(iii)
ice is astonished by water
—Jane Hirshfield, *The Beauty: Poems*

Each time a breath leaves our body, someone dies. With a day's
breathing we inhale at least one molecule from the breath
of every person who has ever lived. When I read this, I knew
that would include you, the one I love; you enter me once a day,
and rest in me the way water sleeps in ice.

Now I dare not exhale, lest you leave. Don't die, you
begged me; memories are so hard to hold. Our life together ended
with a flat line across a screen, a blip, a respirator's hiss,
and a young nurse whispering *he passed* to the doctor who failed
to arrive on time.

He is dead, I wanted to weep. Is it so difficult to say: *He died.*
The light around your body paled, there was a washed translucence
in the air and then—the astonishment of your last breath
brushed my face.

Put the Kettle on

The cup that cheers but does not inebriate,
my grandmother would say, those afternoons
at three while we waited for the water to boil.
They sold her special blend—black, robust—
at a shop on 4th Avenue; after she died
they stocked it until the tea shop closed
and a coffee house opened in its place,
offering herbal infusions for those
with more tepid constitutions.

I can still picture Grannie, who came
from a long line of worriers: in the middle
of a good fret, she assured me, there was nothing
more comforting than a proper cup of tea. Milk
in first (it rendered the tannins insoluble), a dash
of milk which meant a mere splash and nothing
more extravagant. She taught me—it was
presumptuous to pour milk into somebody else's
cup, a slippery slope to murder and beyond.

Next came sugar, at least six heaping teaspoons,
the sugar-spoon engraved with her family crest,
a bloody dagger and *I Mak Sikker* (I Make Sure).
Even from her ebbing bed Grannie insisted
we put the kettle on. When you are in control
of nothing else in your life, you could still make
a cup of tea the way you liked it—strong
enough you wouldn't need faith to walk on it,
sweet enough to float a bullet.

Tending Small Flowers in Spring

My mother, ninety this spring, is fed up
with the deer raiding her garden. It hurts
too much, she says, to try and scare them
away. It hurts to be alive, to have to move
your limbs, to bend down and pull the weeds.
She can no longer kneel and when she falls
she can't get up again. I have known my mother

longer than I've known anyone. She can still
get around well enough to leave
a vase of small flowers—the blue vase
we bought on our last trip to Ireland—
in the guest room when I come home
to stay. She picks last year's pearly everlastings,
what she calls deadery—so tough
even the deer have forsaken them—
that thrive for no reason in the riot of weeds.

Exculpatory Lilies

Good Friday, the day they delivered
that sad bouquet, was the day our cat
ran out on the road and failed to look
both ways. I'd stashed the candy eggs
under the sink, in their pink raffia nests,
safe amongst the household poisons
where the kids had been warned not to go:
on Easter Sunday before first light
I stole outside to hide the loot: the family
of bunnies in gold foil, the high quality
chocolate you insisted on buying—
nothing's too good for my girls! The lilies,
smacking of humility, devotion, had been
for me—your way of saying *sorry, I can stop,
I will lose the needle and spoon today*
but I was finished, I was through, said *sorry*
had been your default setting since the day
we vowed *I do.* I think, now, I was cruel.

The cat darted out, hit the car, staggered back
as far as our front gate; for a second, I thought
she might have been stunned, nothing more,
though the dribble of blood at the corners of her
mouth was a small grief with a life of its own.
I buried her at the bottom of the garden
where I had tossed your exculpatory lilies.

And where I picture them still. *Each new day*
above ground is a hard miracle, you wrote;
I hung on every miraculous breath you took
as I stood outside your door at night, dying
to hear you breathe. In the end, it wasn't me

you turned to, but God: wasn't love meant to be
more pure than faith, more sacred and enduring?
These days I lean heavy into the wind
and the wind's blowing hard.

First Sight

Love before first sight, that's how it was
with you. And now, thirty years later,
I go down to the river, filled with an old
longing. The river might seem unmoved,
but its beauty goes deep, as mysterious
as first love. I whisper the word *love*
to the cold north wind, and the wind
bows its head, ruffles the water's surface.
In the patterns the wind makes across
the black depths, our names, joined.

Rain

> The tears I shed yesterday have become rain.
> —Thich Nhat Hanh

I almost weep for myself,
for this, having to be human.
Did you ever hear of loneliness?
Did you? I let the days enter me.
I let loneliness be the choir
that requires I sing alto
when I wish to be a soprano.
I could reach the high
notes, I promise you, if only
I could learn to breathe.
I don't know how to breathe.
If I breathed I could be rain, I could
fall. How fiercely have you loved
your days? Have you? How few days
are left, what few hours. For now
I know this: *the broken bottles our lives are.*

ROGER REEVES

Best Barbarian

Among the many remarkable poems in *Best Barbarian* is "Journey to Satchidananda" in which the poet writes: "The Japanese call it Kintsugi. / Where the vessel broken, only gold will permit / Its healing. Its history." The beauty of that repair, which does not hide nor erase the evidence of trauma—of history—but transforms it, is the abiding metaphor in this capacious and wide-ranging meditation. At the intersections of history and myth, elegy and celebration, these poems chart the ruptures and violences enacted across time and space—particularly against black humanity—while leaning always toward beauty. Beauty and tenderness abound in this collection that dares to risk both: a brilliant and ambitious book.

Grendel

All lions must lean into something other than a roar:
James Baldwin, for instance, singing *Precious Lord*,
His voice as weary as water broken over his scalp
In a storefront Sanctified Church's baptismal pool
All those years ago when he wanted to be
Somebody's child and on fire in that being. Lord,
I want to be somebody's child and chosen
Water spilling over their scalp, water
Taking the shape of their longing, a deer
Diving into evening traffic and the furrow drawn
In the air over the hood of the car—power
And wanting to be something alive and open.
Lord, I want to be alive and open,
A glimpse of power: the shuffle of a mother's hand
Over a sleeping child's forehead
As if clearing the city's rust from its face
Which we mostly are: a halo of rust,
A glimpse of power—James Baldwin leaning
Into the word *light*, his voice jostling that single grain
In his throat as if he might drop it or
Already has. I am calling to that grain
Of light, to that gap between his teeth
Where the many-of-us fatherless sleep
And bear and be whatever darkness or leaping
Thing we can be. In James Baldwin's mouth,
My difficult beauty, my weak and worn,
My future as any number of angels,
Which is not unlike the beast, Grendel,
Coming out of the wild heaven into the hills
And halls of the mead house at the harpist's call
With absolute prophecy in his breast
And a desire for mercy, for a friend, an end
To drifting in loneliness, and in that coming

Down out of the hills, out of the trees, for once,
Bringing humans the best vision of themselves,
Which, of course, must be slaughtered.

Children Listen

      It turns out however that I was deeply
Mistaken about the end of the world
      The body in flames will not be the body
In flames but just a house fire ignored
      The black sails of that solitary burning
Boat rubbing along the legs of lovers
      Flung into a Roman sky by a carousel
The lovers too sick in their love
      To notice a man drenched in fire on a porch
Or a child aflame mistaken for a dog
      Mistaken for a child running to tell of a bomb
That did not knock before it entered
      In Gaza with its glad tidings of abundant joy
In Kazimierz a god is weeping
      In a window one golden hand raised
Above his head as if he's slipped
      On the slick rag of the future our human
Kindnesses unremarkable as the flies
      Rubbing their legs together while standing
On a slice of cantaloupe Children
      You were never meant to be human
You must be the grass
      You must grow wildly over the graves

Rat Among the Pines

Terror, tonight

Is the moon
Slipping from a rat's gray grasp,

Finding its way back
Into the sky, which is America—

A white moon
Leaning on the night's neck

With its hands in its pocket,
Moon hung calm above

Catastrophe, the police
Breaking the neck of a man

Who had just brushed summer's
First bead of rain from his eye-

Lashes. Who—knocking a Newport
Against a wrist, watching smoke

Break its head against a brick
Wall—is preparing to die

Unaware they are preparing to die.
Heavy the moon, silly the tasking

Of a rat with delaying death.
Terror, tonight

Is the candor of the earth
Where someone is preparing to die

And the earth receives that dying
With its hands in its pockets.

And the moon that once burnt the silk
Hump of a rat, back in the sky.

And my daughter hiding in the rose
Bushes, asking who, who the sirens

Have come to kill. And someone calling
It beautiful—summer, moon—

And someone dying beneath that beauty,
Which is America.

American Landscaping, Philadelphia to Mount Vernon

Who would have thought—too much simultaneity:
The Swan Planters hovering above the wind-beaten
Statue of the Virgin Mary that casts her gaze down
On the Re-Painted Lawn Jockey, his brown face
Spreading out over his white cap, a small rebellion
Or, merely, an inarticulate hand overzealous
In restoring Race back to its place in God after
Winter makes heathen the heaven of horticulture.
This is America calling: the golden pollen of Spring
Blinging every available sedan, stone porch, puddle,
And satin blouse hanging from a smiling white line
Into yellow salvation, or forgetfulness, a black dog,
Antique in its hunger for my daughter's hand through a fence,
My daughter, in her machine and wonder, willing
To give. It is as if every moment is praying
For whatever is above it or just outside of its grasp: the dog
For a hand, the Lawn Jockey holding his absent lantern
Out in front of him for the Virgin whose eyes,
No longer there, Januaried away by the blizzards,
Salt, and wind, stutter with a brown streak
I won't call bird shit but rusted water
Dripping from the corrugated roof above.
Even the flies, in the earliest part of the sentence,
Twitch above the sidewalk as if being accused
Of neglect, infanticide, murder, ending the empire
In order to start another in their own image.
But, what is an empire fashioned in the image of flies?
Mistake: it's not a lantern the Jockey holds
Out in front of him, but a black hitching ring
For masters to tether the tamed because they lack
Mastering, though not the Jockey, who stands on the wind
And paving stones like Jocko Graves, the slave
Of General Washington, who froze to death
Enfolded in snow on the banks of the Delaware River,

His lantern out in front of him awaiting his master's return
As he had been ordered, and Washington, so moved
By Graves' frozen obedience, constructs a statue
Of dead Graves holding a lamp at his plantation
Home in Mount Vernon. Even in death, a slave must
Labor though I knew nothing of these clothes
When, on a Ferris Wheel, overlooking the muddy
Syringed and bottled banks of Philadelphia, I kissed a girl
Through the tin smog and chemical plant perfume
And carried that kiss through the year, touching newspaper,
Edges of blankets, the backs of hamburger buns
To my lips to remember the dimming summer
Sheepishly backing out of a door it hurriedly burst through.
Only in America will the sons and daughters of slaves
Kiss the sons and daughters of their masters
And remember it as an opportunity to be human.

After the Funeral

A white cat has come to sit on the backside of slaughter,
    To sit on a white bull bearing a necklace of pomegranates.
The cat has come not as any witness to a crucifixion
    Or a coronation, not as angel or symbol of some comfort
Creature, some benign break in the dying,
    But as human wish, as distraction from suffering.

My human wish: to keep my father's schizophrenia
    In his casket, to keep *that* below the earth, one from another,
Now and forever. In season and out.
    From mountain to mountain. In the trees and after. Amen.
Everything has come back to prayer, sitting in that delay,
    'Harrowing the fixities,' my father in me, in my clock,
My hoof, my feather, in the sprawling
    Armature and stars of I am. Lord, am I worthy?

Have I devotion? What body built? Of flood, of cancer,
    Of winter, of woman—Lord,
I pray as I've been taught—to keep nothing
    From my tongue, its palm, its golden mind
So it bees and be's with whatever it be's—rose, rain—Lord,
    Even her, even her who rises from this bed,
The naked two-ness of her filling the room such that she becomes the room—
    Lord, am I ready?

How shall I bear the coming madness if it is come?
    What disaster will I deliver to my daughter?
My human wish: distraction: a white cat,
    Balanced on the backside of a bull, slaughter
Far off, this delay, Lord, this delay I offer
    Because I own neither houses nor land, have not a hundred heads
Of cattle or of State grazing on grain in a golden-green field.
    Keep this coming distant, this sickness underground,

And if Lord I am, if I am to bear madness,
    Become the father who scratches the raw earth
With his hoof and snout, plowing the field
    As ox or ass because the mind says, *go, go*
Into the pasture not as ox or as ass but go, Ox,
    Go, Ass, then Lord, let me into the field, but make,
Lord, Diviner of the snowflake and master of fragments,
    A light, a golden light in a tree,

And there, have my daughter stare at its working
    The darkness in the green, in the leaves and red blooms,
While I, behind her, lick the tines of a fence
    And leap in the dust in front of a white cat
That has become my master, that I follow
    Out to a white bull bearing a necklace of pomegranates.

Drapetomania, Or James Baldwin As an Improvisation

Absent bounty, anarchic and asymptotic,
Bedlam banked as beauty, captive cuckolding
Capital and its camel-faced captor, master, the
Devil is in the dove's details, even doves
Exist as furious, fragile, violent and decent
(Which could describe anyone at all, including
Freedom), even freedom exists, god's good
Hostage, haint haunting the hootenanny,
If, as in the *if-only-you-knew* of Patti
LaBelle sung in the broken-bottle falsetto
Of an uncle laid out on the bottom step
Of summer, sobriety, and Miss Such-
A-Much's sliding-away love, jaundiced
As James Baldwin's good and lovely dying

Eye; James Baldwin existed as an improvisation,
Knuckles calling for a Newport to knock, light,
Lift, lustrous and otherwise, Malcom X
Marking X where it is he loved the poor—
Everywhere, everywhere, which is where
Detroit is red, recalcitrant, panther,
Battlefield where the moon says I love you,
Naysayers, narcoleptics, no-names, nap-
Deprived, on time and out of time, queer—
The color of how we made it over empire,
Petulance, pneumonia, the nubs, neck pain,
Needles nosing in our nana's uterus,
Notices of eviction, *Notes on the State*
Of Virginia and how negroes ain't shit

But buckra-beaters, bears, butches, bull-
Daggers and welfare queens, sometimes, cute,
Coons, country, cow-tipped, downward dogs, earth-
Empty, flies, fungible, freaks, gutter-rough,

Hasslers, hijinks, handsome in harnesses,
Ignorant as ice, juridical conundrums
Nappy kitchens, kaput, light and heavy
Work, madness's martyr and minor
Mayhem, misled Drapetomaniacs,
Nothing worth noting, a now made then,
Occult and organized as outlandish,
Pariahs, presidents, quarrelsome,
Roustabouts and randy, skit, scat, and shat,
Tercentennial and tough-going

Mulattoes, tragic and otherwise,
Translated as any number of ain'ts,
Apocalypses, unaffiliated
And unctuous, various and varicose,
Vestibules of the new world—remnants
Of light from a cigarette balanced
Between the knuckles of James Baldwin's hand,
Leopard, the remnants of light exist,
Wayward as any many and less
Where the moon fields the night, and the shadow
Of a boy running through an unplowed field
Turns the earth, turns the earth round, gold,
Back against the bedlam of being hunted by any
X, Y, and Z; you, you who survived this earth.

Journey to Satchidananda

Alice Coltrane, her harp, fills in the cracks of me
With gold. The Japanese call it Kintsugi.
Where the vessel broken, only gold will permit
Its healing. Its history. It's *How the Stars Understand
Us*, lemon flowers on the skin of the earth,
Mosquito filled with the blood that sirens its fat,
Long life. Who isn't dying to leave this house,
To go masked only in the shadow of one's animal-
Breathing, lonesome, unprotected, *knowing
Nothing lives as foreignness* or death,
That the black dog with the sword in his mouth
Passing from house to house will not bring its itch,
Its ticks and locks clogging our lungs, a permanent
Quarantine—nothing that a little gold
Melted to ichor and spilled into the veins
Won't seam. Everything is a blue divergence
On a harp, the red bells in the purple
Crepe myrtle this morning forgetting
That soon they will be the corpses the spring
Tree kneels to observe. No, no, they remember,
As everything dying remembers its mother's
Name. *Say your mother's name.* Not for power
But for the glimpse of power, to be more
Than a hesitation, gold filling in the cracks,
A window thrown open for no other reason
Than to continue a blue feeling, nothing
Needed other than this devotion to darkness,
A Fire Gotten Brighter, my daughter holding
My small name in her mouth, light-broken
Beloved, my daughter—a window thrown
Open—her voice, gold filling in the cracked
Basketball court of me, announcing *all
Nature, all nature will be dead for life soon.*

OCEAN VUONG

Time Is a Mother

Time Is a Mother is a breathtaking poetry book that rediscovers the voice of loss and the fragile layers of identity. Vuong's writing is visceral, shaped like a relief map of unpredictable past and present. One of the most striking aspects of his poetry is the way in which he captures the passage of time, placing the seed of new worlds into time's womb. He reflects on the ways in which memory becomes our body, and how the past can walk alongside us and open the doors of non-inherited grief and love. *Time Is a Mother* was written after the death of his mother—his silent muse and protector from the sharp edges of new borders and languages. He once said: "As a woman of color, an Asian woman, in the world, she taught me how to be vigilant. How people's faces, posture, tone, could be read. She taught me how to make everything legible when language was not." Her death opened the window of eternal dialogue between them. Behind the shadows of loss, grief, and abandonment, his poetry reflects the strong echo of a ritualistic celebration of life and hope.

The Bull

He stood alone in the backyard, so dark
the night purpled around him.
I had no choice. I opened the door
& stepped out. Wind
in the branches. He watched me with kerosene
-blue eyes. *What do you want?* I asked, forgetting I had
no language. He kept breathing,
to stay alive. I was a boy—
which meant I was a murderer
of my childhood. & like all murderers, my god
was stillness. My god, he was still
there. Like something prayed for
by a man with no mouth. The green-blue lamp
swirled in its socket. I didn't
want him. I didn't want him to
be beautiful—but needing beauty
to be more than hurt gentle
enough to hold, I
reached for him. I reached—not the bull—
but the depths. Not an answer but
an entrance the shape of
an animal. Like me.

Skinny Dipping

some boys
  have ghosted
from this high

but I wanna go
  down on you
anyway to leap

from the bridge
  I've made
of my wrongs look

they lied to us
  no one here
was ever ugly look

if you see
  me then
I prayed

correctly I leapt
  from the verb
taking off

my best shirt
  this rag & rage
a tulip too late

in summer's teeth
  like the blade
in a guillotine I won't

pick a side
          my name a past
tense where I left

my hands
          for good oh
it should be

enough to live
          & die alone
with music on

your tongue
          to jump from
anywhere & make it

home
          to be warm & full of
nothing oh

I kept my hope
          -blue Vans on
this whole time

to distract you
          from my flat ass
did it work oh

my people my people
          I thought
the fall would

kill me
          but it only
made me real

The Last Prom Queen in Antarctica

It's true I'm all talk & a French tuck
but so what. Like the wind, I ride
my own life. Neon light electric
in the wet part of roadkill
on the street where I cut my teeth
on the good sin. I want to
take care of our planet
because I need a beautiful
graveyard. It's true I'm not a writer
but a faucet underwater. When the flood comes
I'll raise my hand so they know
who to shoot. The sky flashes. The sea
yearns. I myself
am hell. Everyone's here. Sometimes
I go to parties just to dangle my feet
out of high windows, among people.
This boy crying in his car
after his shift at McDonald's
on Easter Sunday. The way
he wipes his eyes with his shirt
as the big trucks blare
off the interstate. My favorite
kind of darkness is the one
inside us, I want to tell him.
&: I like the way your apron
makes it look like you're ready
for war. I too am ready for war.
Given another chance, I'd pick the life
where I play the piano
in a room with no roof. Broken keys, Bach
sonata like footsteps fast
down the stairs as
my father chases my mother
through New England's endless

leaves. Maybe I saw a boy
in a black apron crying in a Nissan
the size of a monster's coffin & knew
I could never be straight. Maybe,
like you, I was one of those people
who loves the world most
when I'm rock-bottom in my fast car
going nowhere.

Waterline

If I should wake & the Ark
the Ark already
gone

If there was one shivering thing
at my side

If the snow in his hair
was all that was left

of the fire

If we ran through the orchard
with our mouths
wide open

& still too small
for amen

If I nationed myself
in the shadow
of a colossal wave

If only to hold on
by opening—
by kingdom come

give me this one
eighth day
let me enter
this nearly-gone *yes*

the way death enters
anything fully
without a trace

Scavengers

           Your body wakes
into its quiet rattle
              Ropes & ropes
    How quickly the animal
empties
      We're alone again
          with spent mouths

Two trout gasping
                on a June shore
Side by side, I see
        what I came for, behind

your iris: a tiny mirror
               I stare
into its silver syllable
        where a fish with my face
twitches once
     then gones

           The fisherman
              suddenly a boy
with too much to carry

Tell Me Something Good

You are standing in the minefield again.
Someone who is dead now

told you it is where you will learn
to dance. Snow on your lips like a salted

cut, you leap between your deaths, black as god's
periods. Your arms cleaving

the wind. You are something made, then made
to survive—which means you are somebody's son.

Which means if you open your eyes, you'll be back in
that house, under a blanket printed with yellow sailboats.

Your mother's boyfriend, bald head ringed with red
hair, a planet on fire, kneeling

by your bed again. Air of whiskey & crushed
Oreos. Snow falling through the window: ash returned

from a failed fable. His spilled-ink hand
on your chest. & you keep dancing inside the minefield—

motionless. The curtains fluttering. Honeyed light
beneath the door. His breath. His wet blue face: earth

spinning in no one's orbit. & you want someone to say
Hey...Hey,
I think your dancing is gorgeous. A two-step to die for,

darling. You want someone to say all this
is long ago. That one night, very soon, you'll pack a bag

with your favorite paperback & your mother's .45,
that the surest shelter was always the thoughts

above your head. That it's fair—it has to be—
how our hands hurt us, then give us

the world. How you can love the world
until there's nothing left to love

but yourself. Then you can stop.
Then you can walk away—back into the fog

-walled minefield, where the vein in your neck adores you
to zero. You can walk away. You can be nothing

& still breathing. Believe me.

Almost Human

It's been a long time since my body.
Unbearable, I put it down
on the earth the way my old man
rolled dice. It's been a long time since
time. But I had weight back there. Had substance
& sinew, damage you could see
by looking between your hands & hearing
blood. It was called reading, they told me,
too late. But too late. I red. I made a killing
in language & was surrounded
by ghosts. I used my arsenal
of defunct verbs & broke
into a library of second chances,
the ER. Where they bandaged
my head, even as the black letters
kept seeping through,
like this. Back there, I couldn't
get the boys to look at me
even in my best jean jacket.
It was 2006 or 1865 or .327.
What a time to be alive! they said,
this time louder, more assault rifles.
Did I tell you? I come from a people of sculptors
whose masterpiece was rubble. We
tried. Indecent, tongue-tied, bowl-cut & diabetic,
I had a feeling. The floorboards creaked
as I wept motionless by the rehab window.
If words, as they claimed, had no weight
in our world, why did we keep
sinking, Doctor—I mean
Lord—why did the water swallow
our almost human hands
as we sang? Like this.

Woodworking at the End of the World

In a field, after everything, a streetlamp
shining on a patch of grass.

Having just come back to life, I lay down under its warmth
& waited for a way.

That's when the boy appeared, lying next to me.

He was wearing a Ninja Turtles t-shirt
from another era, the colors faraway.

I recognized his eyes: black buttons salvaged from the coat
I used to cover my mother's face, at the end.

Why do you exist? I wanted to know.

I felt the crickets around us but couldn't hear them.

A chapel on the last day of war.

That's how quiet he was.

The town I had walked from was small & American.

If I stayed on my knees, it would keep all my secrets.

When we heard the woodcutters coming closer, destroying
the past to build the future, the boy started to cry.

But the voice, the voice that came out
was an old man's.

I reached into my pocket
but the gun was gone.

I must've dropped it while burying my language
farther up the road.

It's okay, the boy said at last. *I forgive you.*

Then he kissed me as if returning a porcelain shard
to my cheek.

Shaking, I turned to him. I turned
& found, crumpled on the grass, the faded red shirt.

I put it over my face & stayed very still—like my mother
at the end.

Then it came to me, my life. I remembered my life
the way an ax handle, mid-swing, remembers the tree.

& I was free.

THE POETS

ROBYN CRESWELL teaches comparative literature at Yale University and is a consulting editor for poetry at Farrar, Straus and Giroux. He is the author of *City of Beginnings: Poetic Modernism in Beirut* and contributes regularly to the *New York Review of Books*.

IMAN MERSAL is the author of five books of poems and a collection of essays, *How to Mend: Motherhood and Its Ghosts*. In English translation, her poems have appeared in the *Paris Review*, the *New York Review of Books*, the *Nation*, and other publications. Her most recent prose work, *Traces of Enayat*, received the Sheikh Zayed Book Award for Literature in 2021. She is a professor of Arabic language and literature at the University of Alberta, Canada.

ADA LIMÓN is the author of six books of poetry, including *The Carrying*, which won the National Book Critics Circle Award and was named a finalist for the PEN/Jean Stein Book Award. Her book *Bright Dead Things* was nominated for the National Book Award, the National Book Critics Circle Award, and the Kingsley Tufts Poetry Award. Her work has been supported most recently by a Guggenheim Fellowship. She is the new host of American Public Media's weekday poetry podcast, *The Slowdown*. She grew up in Sonoma, California, and now lives in Lexington, Kentucky, where she writes and teaches remotely. She is the 24th Poet Laureate of the United States.

SUSAN MUSGRAVE lives off Canada's West Coast, on Haida Gwaii, where she owns and manages Copper Beech House. She teaches in University of British Columbia's Optional Residency School of Creative Writing. She has published more than thirty books and been nominated or received awards in six categories—poetry, novels, non-fiction, food writing, editing, and books for children. The high point of her literary career was finding her name in the index of *Montreal's Irish Mafia*.

ROGER REEVES is the author of *King Me* and the recipient of a National Endowment for the Arts fellowship, a Ruth Lilly and Dorothy Sargent Rosenberg Poetry Fellowship from the Poetry Foundation, and a 2015 Whiting Award, among other honours. His work has appeared in *Poetry*, the *New Yorker*, the *Paris Review*, and elsewhere. He lives in Austin, Texas.

OCEAN VUONG is the author of the critically acclaimed poetry collection *Night Sky with Exit Wounds* and the *New York Times* best-selling novel *On Earth We're Briefly Gorgeous*. A recipient of the 2019 MacArthur "Genius Grant," he is also the winner of the Whiting Award and the T. S. Eliot Prize. His writings have been featured in the *Atlantic*, *Harper's Magazine*, the *Nation*, the *New Republic*, the *New Yorker*, and the *New York Times*. Born in Saigon, Vietnam, he currently lives in Northampton, Massachusetts.

THE JUDGES

GREGORY SCOFIELD is Métis of Cree, Scottish, and European-immigrant descent whose ancestry can be traced to the Métis community of Kinosota, Manitoba. He has taught creative writing and First Nations and Métis literature at Laurentian University, Brandon University, Emily Carr University of Art + Design, and the Alberta University of the Arts. He currently holds the position of associate professor in the Department of Writing at the University of Victoria. Scofield won the Dorothy Livesay Poetry Prize in 1994 for his debut collection, *The Gathering: Stones for the Medicine Wheel*, and has since published seven further volumes of poetry, including *Witness, I Am*. He has served as writer-in-residence at the University of Manitoba, the University of Winnipeg, and Memorial University of Newfoundland. He is the recipient of the Queen's Diamond Jubilee Medal (2012) and, most recently, the Writers' Trust of Canada Latner Poetry Prize (2016), which is awarded to a mid-career poet in recognition of a remarkable body of work. Further to writing and teaching, Scofield is also a skilled bead-worker, and he creates in the medium of traditional Métis arts. He continues to assemble a collection of mid- to late-nineteenth-century Cree-Métis artifacts, which are used as learning and teaching pieces. Scofield's first memoir, *Thunder Through My Veins* (Doubleday Canada/Anchor Books), was republished in fall 2019.

NIKOLA MADZIROV (poet, essayist, translator) was born in 1973 in Strumica, R.Macedonia, in a family of war refugees from the Balkan Wars. When he was eighteen, the collapse of Yugoslavia prompted a shift in his sense of identity—as a writer reinventing himself in a country that felt new but was still nourished by deeply rooted historical traditions. His poems are translated into more than forty languages. The book *Relocated Stone* (2007) was given the East European Hubert Burda poetry award and the most prestigious Macedonian poetry award, the Miladinov Brothers, at Struga Poetry Evenings. Other recognitions include the Studentski Zbor award for best poetry debut and the Xu Zhimo Silver Leaf award for European poetry at King's College, Cambridge, in the UK. American composers Oliver Lake, Michael League, Becca Stevens, and Du Yun have composed music based on Madzirov's poems. He was granted several international fellowships: International Writing Program at University of Iowa, DAAD in Berlin, Marguerite Yourcenar in France, and Civitella Ranieri in Italy. Nikola Madzirov is one of the coordinators of the international poetry network Lyrikline, based in Berlin. He edited the Macedonian edition of the *Anthology of World's Poetry: XX and XXI Century*. His book in English *Remnants of Another Age* was published in the US by BOA Editions and in the UK by Bloodaxe Books.

NATASHA TRETHEWEY served two terms as the 19th Poet Laureate of the United States (2012–14). She is the author of five collections of poetry, including *Native Guard* (2006)—for which she was awarded the 2007 Pulitzer Prize—and, most recently, *Monument: Poems New and Selected* (2018); a book of non-fiction, *Beyond Katrina: A Meditation on the Mississippi Gulf Coast* (2010); and a memoir, *Memorial Drive* (2020) an instant *New York Times* bestseller. She is the recipient of fellowships from the Academy of American Poets, the National Endowment for the Arts, the Guggenheim Foundation, the Rockefeller Foundation, the Beinecke Library at Yale, and the Radcliffe Institute for Advanced Study at Harvard. She is a fellow of the American Academy of Arts and Sciences, the American Academy of Arts and Letters, and the American Philosophical Society. In 2017 she received the Heinz Award for Arts and Humanities. A Chancellor of the Academy of American

Poets since 2019, Trethewey was awarded the 2020 Rebekah Johnson Bobbitt National Prize in Poetry for Lifetime Achievement from the Library of Congress. In 2022 she was the William B. Hart Poet in Residence at the American Academy in Rome. Currently, she is Board of Trustees Professor of English at Northwestern University.

ACKNOWLEDGEMENTS

The publisher thanks the following for their kind permission to reprint the work contained in this volume:

"Just sleeping," "Visits," "Little lockers," "It seems I inherit the dead," "They tear down my family home," "Why did she come?," "CV," and "The book of desire" from *The Threshold* by Iman Mersal, translated by Robyn Creswell, are reprinted by permission of Farrar, Straus and Giroux.

"Give Me This," "Forsythia," "The First Fish," "It's the Season I Often Mistake," "The Hurting Kind," "Against Nostalgia," and "The End of Poetry" from *The Hurting Kind* by Ada Limón are reprinted by permission of Corsair Poetry.

"The True Beginning of Loneliness," "Postscript," "The Way Water Sleeps," "Put the Kettle on," "Tending Small Flowers in Spring," "Exculpatory Lilies," "First Sight," and "Rain" from *Exculpatory Lilies* by Susan Musgrave are reprinted by permission of McClelland & Stewart.

"Grendel," "Children Listen," "Rat Among the Pines," "American Landscaping, Philadelphia to Mount Vernon," "After the Funeral," "Drapetomania, or James Baldwin As an Improvisation," and "Journey to Satchidananda" from *Best Barbarian* by Roger Reeves are reprinted by permission of W. W. Norton.

GRIFFIN POETRY PRIZE ANTHOLOGY 2023

The best books of poetry published in English are honoured each year with the $130,000 Griffin Poetry Prize, one of the world's most prestigious and richest international literary awards. Since 2001 this annual prize has acted as a tremendous spur to interest in and recognition of poetry, focusing worldwide attention on the formidable talent of poets writing in English and works in translation. And each year the editor of the *Griffin Poetry Prize Anthology* gathers the work of the extraordinary poets shortlisted for the award and introduces us to some of the finest poems in their collections.

This year, editor and prize juror Gregory Scofield's selections from the shortlist include poems from Iman Mersal's *The Threshold*, translated by Robyn Creswell (Farrar, Straus and Giroux), Ada Limón's *The Hurting Kind* (Corsair Poetry), Susan Musgrave's *Exculpatory Lilies* (McClelland & Stewart), Roger Reeves's *Best Barbarian* (W. W. Norton), and Ocean Vuong's *Time Is a Mother* (Cape Poetry, and Penguin Press).

In choosing the 2023 shortlist, prize jurors Gregory Scofield, Nikola Madzirov, and Natasha Trethewey each read 602 books of poetry, including 54 translations from 20 languages, submitted by 229 publishers from 20 different countries. The jurors also wrote the citations that introduce the five poets' nominated works.